GETTING TO KN
THE U.S. PRESIDE

CHESTER A.
ARTHUR

TWENTY-FIRST PRESIDENT
1881 – 1885

WRITTEN AND ILLUSTRATED BY MIKE VENEZIA

CHILDREN'S PRESS®
A DIVISION OF SCHOLASTIC INC.
NEW YORK   TORONTO   LONDON   AUCKLAND   SYDNEY
MEXICO CITY   NEW DELHI   HONG KONG
DANBURY, CONNECTICUT

Reading Consultant: Nanci R. Vargus, Ed.D., Assistant Professor, School of Education, University of Indianapolis

Historical Consultant: Marc J. Selverstone, Ph.D., Assistant Professor, Miller Center of Public Affairs, University of Virginia

Photographs © 2006: Corbis Images: 3 (Ole Peter Hansen Balling), 27, 32 (Bettmann), 13 (August Kollner/Museum of the City of New York), 14; Library of Congress: 8, 22, 24, 25; North Wind Picture Archives: 6, 7; Superstock, Inc./Currier & Ives/Library of Congress, Washington, D.C.: 20; The Art Archive/Picture Desk/Culver Pictures: 29; U.S. Naval Historical Center: 31; White House Historical Association/Library of Congress (617): 28.

Colorist for illustrations: Dave Ludwig

Library of Congress Cataloging-in-Publication Data

Venezia, Mike.
  Chester A. Arthur / written and illustrated by Mike Venezia.
    p. cm. — (Getting to know the U.S. presidents)
  ISBN 0-516-22626-6 (lib bdg.) 0-516-25401-4 (pbk.)
  1. Arthur, Chester Alan, 1829-1886—Juvenile literature. 2.
Presidents—United States—Biography—Juvenile literature. I. Title.
  E692.V46 2006
  973.8'4'092–dc22
                                    2005012084

1 2 3 4 5 6 7 8 9 10 R 15 14 13 12 11 10 09 08 07 06

A portrait of President Chester A. Arthur

Chester A. Arthur was the twenty-first president of the United States. He was born in Fairfield, Vermont, on October 5, 1829. Chet, as his friends called him, loved politics. He had lots of important government jobs throughout his life. Even so, Chet Arthur never expected to become president.

Chester A. Arthur was proud to have been
chosen as President James Garfield's vice
president. It was the perfect job for him.
He looked forward to leading the meetings
of the U.S. Senate and attending lots of

government ceremonies and dinners. Chester A. Arthur always loved having a good time. Then something happened that shocked the nation and changed Vice President Arthur's life overnight!

An illustration showing the assassination of President Garfield

On July 2, 1881, an insane man shot President James Garfield. Garfield died about ten weeks later, on September 19, 1881. The next morning, Chester A. Arthur was sworn in as president of the United States.

Many people didn't trust their new president. In the past, Chet had held jobs at

Chester A. Arthur was sworn in as president at his New York home soon after President Garfield's death.

and belonged to political organizations run by dishonest, crooked men. Many people worried that President Arthur's old friends would try to control him. A nervous nation waited to see how Chester A. Arthur would handle his new job.

Reverend William Arthur, Chester A. Arthur's father

There isn't a lot of information about Chester A. Arthur's childhood. He never talked much about growing up in Vermont and New York. Also, near the end of his life, he burned all his private notes and papers.

Chester A. Arthur was the son of a preacher. His father, Reverend William Arthur, was an abolitionist. He hated the idea of slavery and wasn't afraid to argue with church members who disagreed with him.

Reverend Arthur was hot tempered and would often interrupt his sermon to embarrass or insult anyone who wasn't paying attention. Because of Reverend Arthur's attitude, Chet and his family ended up moving seven times while he was growing up.

Reverend Arthur schooled his children at home when they were young. One thing that Chet never forgot was his father's lessons about the cruelty of slavery. When Chet was a little older, he attended a private school, and then Union College in Schenectady, New York.

After college, Chet decided to become a lawyer. He traveled to New York City to work and study at a well-known law office. New York was the nation's largest and busiest city. Chet saw how some people there lived in great luxury. He hoped that someday he, too, would be able to afford fine clothes, the best restaurants, and have his own horse-drawn carriage.

Chet worked for a man named Erastus Culver. Erastus was an abolitionist. He hated slavery as much as Chet did. Mr. Culver was happy to help Chet study for his law exam.

In 1854, Chester A. Arthur passed his law exam. He was then invited to become a partner in Mr. Culver's law firm. Soon Chet was working on some important cases defending the rights of African Americans.

This illustration shows streetcars in New York City in the mid-1800s. During that time, Chester Arthur won an important case upholding the right of African Americans to sit in any seat on a New York City streetcar.

In one case, Chet represented an African-American schoolteacher named Elizabeth Jennings. Elizabeth had been forced out of her seat in the "whites only" section of a streetcar. Chet fought for Elizabeth Jennings' right to sit wherever she wanted. He won the court case, and all New York streetcar companies had to get rid of their seating restrictions forever.

Ellen Herndon Arthur

Chester A. Arthur was happy to have won an important court case. It was an exciting time for him. Not only was he becoming well known as a lawyer, but he also met his future wife, Ellen Herndon, during this time. Ellen, also known as Nell, was from a wealthy Virginia family. She often traveled to New York to visit relatives and sing in choral groups.

Nell's father was a famous sea captain. Captain Herndon led an expedition to explore the unknown parts of the Amazon River in South America. After dating for a while, Chet and Nell decided to get married. Later on, the couple became known for giving the best and most elegant parties in New York City.

As busy as Chet was, he also became involved in politics. He joined a new political group, the Republican Party. There was another group, called the Democratic Party, but Chet liked the Republicans because they were against slavery.

Chet noticed that people who worked hard and became leaders in political parties could make lots of money. Party members who helped get a candidate elected would often be rewarded with a cushy government job.

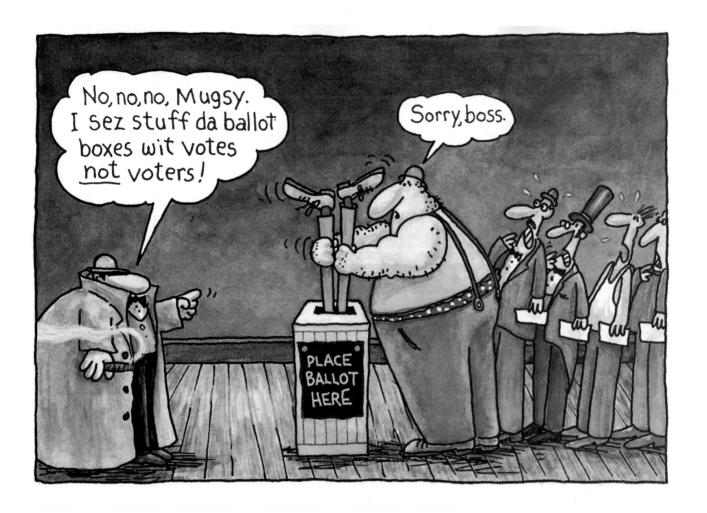

In return, thousands of workers promised to give part of their salary back to their party bosses. This arrangement was known as the spoils system. Both Republican and Democratic Party leaders would do almost anything to get their candidate elected. They even stuffed ballot boxes with made-up votes, or hired thugs to keep their opponents from voting!

In 1861, when the Civil War began, Chet was rewarded with an important job. Chet had worked hard to get some Republican candidates elected. He was put in charge of organizing all the volunteer soldiers in the New York area who would be fighting in the war.

It was Chet's job to make sure hundreds of thousands of men had food, supplies, places to live, and transportation to battle areas. It was an awesomely huge and difficult job. Chester A. Arthur impressed everyone by making things run as smoothly as possible. He especially impressed his Republican Party bosses.

After the Civil War ended, Chet was rewarded with another government job. Some people said it was the best job in the country. He was put in charge of the New York Customs House. Chet got a huge salary as collector of the Port of New York. Now he was able to live the way he had always dreamed.

As collector of the Port of New York, Chester A. Arthur supervised the collection of taxes and fees on all goods that came into New York Harbor (above).

The Customs House collected taxes and fees on all goods or products shipped into New York Harbor. The only problem was that the Customs House was filled with workers who had been given jobs as favors. Many of them were unqualified, lazy, and crooked. They found it easy to steal some of the tax money for themselves.

Rutherford B. Hayes

Chester A. Arthur never had a problem with the spoils system. He thought it was a normal way of doing business. The people who received jobs and favors didn't have a problem with the spoils system, either. Eventually, however, the public became fed up with the thousands of unqualified workers who were making lots of money in government jobs. In 1877, President Rutherford B. Hayes began an investigation to find out just exactly what was going on at the New York Customs House.

Although Chet himself was never accused of doing anything wrong, he was criticized for giving out jobs to his Republican friends. President Hayes ended up forcing Chet to resign. It was an embarrassing low point in Chester A. Arthur's career.

A campaign poster from the 1880 presidential election

Fortunately for Chet, two years later, in 1880, the Republican Party chose him as James Garfield's vice-presidential running mate. James and Chet won a close election. James Garfield wasn't president for long, though. Only four months into his term, President Garfield was shot. He died ten weeks later.

When Chester A. Arthur took over as president, people were worried he would continue using the spoils system to help his friends. President Arthur ended up surprising everyone, however.

Many people assumed that President Arthur would continue the spoils system. This 1881 political cartoon shows the new president as a magician who would need to throw out "promises" of political jobs to keep politicians happy.

Not only was he careful to hire skilled, honest people, he also signed a bill called the Pendleton Act. This law helped put an end to the spoils system. Now workers would have to apply for federal government jobs and take an exam to make sure they knew what they were doing. The Republicans were furious. They couldn't believe their old friend wasn't going to be doing favors for them anymore.

Chester A. Arthur had decided to take the job of president very seriously. He did his best to run his administration in an honest way for the good of the American people.

President Chester A. Arthur

Unfortunately, Arthur's wife, Nell, died before she could see her husband become president of the United States. To keep himself busy after work, President Arthur threw some of the most elegant parties in Washington, D.C. He always served the finest food and hired the best orchestras to play for his guests.

In 1882, President Arthur hired designer Louis Tiffany to redecorate the White House. This 1889 photograph shows Tiffany's changes to the Blue Room of the White House.

President Arthur fishing in New York in 1882

When Chester had first moved into the White House, he was shocked by how run-down it was. He knew the shabby White House wouldn't do for his fancy parties. He immediately hired Louis Tiffany, the best designer in New York City, to redo the entire executive mansion.

When President Arthur wasn't busy doing his job as president, throwing parties, and fixing up the White House, he spent as much time fishing as he could. It was his favorite sport.

Chester A. Arthur served for only one four-year term. During that time, he did everything he could to limit the spoils system and prevent greedy government leaders from using the public's money for their own benefit.

President Arthur also noticed that the United States Navy had been neglected for many years. It was in a real mess, filled with

President Arthur improved the U.S. Navy by authorizing the building of modern metal-clad warships like these.

old-fashioned, run-down wooden ships. He pushed Congress to find money to build new steel steam-powered ships. Thanks to President Arthur, the U.S. Navy would someday become the best in the world.

President Arthur picnicking with a friend in the woods

Chester A. Arthur didn't run for a second term. He knew he had made too many enemies in the Republican Party by doing things his own way. He also had kept a secret. He had a serious kidney disease, and knew he wouldn't be healthy enough to serve another term. Chester A. Arthur died on November 18, 1886, less than two years after he left the White House.

Chester A. Arthur turned out to be a surprisingly good president. His confidence, honesty, and good nature kept the nation running smoothly after a national tragedy.